BEARS

EYES ON NATURE™

BEARS

Written by
Donald Olson

kidsbooks®
Incorporated

Scientific Consultant:
Gary Brown
National Park Ranger
and Bear-Management Specialist

Photo credits:

Tom & Pat Leeson—Pages 6-9, 12, 14, 15, 18-19, 22, 23, 24-27, 29
Michael Francis/Wildlife Collection—Pages 6, 23
Gary Schultz/Wildlife Collection—Pages 7, 23
Martin Harvey/Wildlife Collection—Page 8
John Giustina/Wildlife Collection—Pages 9, 19
Tom Vezo/Wildlife Collection—Page 14
Jack Swenson/Wildlife Collection—Page 14
Dean Lee/Wildlife Collection—Page 27
Robert Lankinen/Wildlife Collection—Pages 20, 21
Henry Holdsworth/Wildlife Collection—Page 25
Ken Lucas/Visuals Unlimited—Page 10
Tom Edwards/Visuals Unlimited—Page 7
William J. Weber/Visuals Unlimited—Page 8
Erwin C. "Bud" Nielsen/Visuals Unlimited—Page 17
Joe McDonald/Visuals Unlimited—Pages 17, 19, 25
Johnny Johnson/DRK—Cover; Pages 6, 10, 12, 13, 16, 20-21
Wayne Lynch/DRK—Pages 6, 9, 10, 13, 18, 21, 22, 28-29
Belinda Wright /DRK—Page 8
Stephen J. Krasemann/DRK—Cover; Pages 11, 15
Fred Bruemmer/DRK—Page 11
Leonard Lee Rue III/DRK—Page 16
Tom and Pat Leeson/DRK—Cover
John W. Matthews/DRK—Page 28
Dwight R. Kuhn/DRK—Page 28
Mike & Lisa Husar/DRK—End Pages
Will Regan/International Stock—Page 15
Ron Sanford/International Stock—Page 16
Mark Newman/International Stock—Pages 19, 20, 21
Wide World Photos—Page 29
Susan Lang—Pages 26-27
Lynn M. Stone—Page 24
Zig Leszczynski—Pages 9, 13, 18, 25
Breck P. Kent—Pages 7, 10, 17, 28-29

Copyright © 1997
Kidsbooks, Inc.
3535 West Peterson Ave.
Chicago, IL 60659

Manufactured in the United States of America

WILD BEARS

These amazing creatures are some of the largest land animals on earth. One of nature's wildest wonders, bears swim, climb, run at surprisingly high speeds, and travel great distances in one day.

This fun-loving grizzly enjoys a roll in a field of berries. ▶

WALKING UPRIGHT ▼

A bear usually walks on all fours. But a curious bear will stand up on its back legs to get a better view or to pull down food from above. To defend itself, a bear will rear up and lash out with its massive paws.

NOT TOO CLOSE

People like to think of bears as cute and cuddly. But bears like to stay far away from people. If startled or provoked, a bear may even attack.

◀ BIG DIET

Bears are big eaters. They are classified as *carnivores,* or meat-eaters, but all have a diet that includes plants. They may also dine on honey, mushrooms, and many other things.

6

► Through bear talk, cubs learn from their mother.

▼ Brown bears roar when they're really angry.

NOT A BEAR
The Australian koala bear is not a member of the bear family at all. A marsupial like the kangaroo, the koala carries and nurses its young in a stomach pouch.

CHATTER ▲
Although they are fairly quiet, bears do communicate with sound. They growl when threatened and hum when content. They even whine and cry when they're upset.

LIVING ALONE
Bears rule wherever they live. Their only enemies, besides people, are other bears. Solitary creatures, they usually avoid one another. Only when it's time to mate do adult males and females get together. A mother bear, however, may spend a couple of years with her cubs.

BEAR COUNTRY

Ever wonder if there are bears living nearby? They might be! Bears can be found on all continents except Africa, Antarctica, and Australia. There are eight living species, which come in a variety of colors.

BROWN BEAR

Found in Europe, in Asia as far south as India, in western Canada, Alaska, and parts of the western United States, brown bears have the greatest range of all. They are also some of the largest bears, weighing over 800 pounds on average and measuring up to 10 feet from nose to tail.

ASIATIC BLACK BEAR

The Asiatic black bear lives in brushlands and forests throughout Asia, including Japan and the island of Taiwan.

BLACK BEAR

The tree-climbing black bear inhabits forests, swamps, and wooded mountains from Alaska and Canada down to Mexico and Florida.

POLAR BEAR

As wintry white as the ice and snow of the North Pole, the polar bear inhabits Arctic areas in Norway, Greenland, Russia, Canada, and Alaska.

SLOTH BEAR

The sloth bear lives throughout the Indian subcontinent, from Nepal and Bhutan down to Sri Lanka. A fairly small bear, it has a white or yellow "necklace" on its black chest.

SPECTACLED BEAR

There's only one bear that lives in South America, and that's the spectacled bear. This unique creature, which gets its name from the markings around its eyes, roams along the Andes Mountains in Venezuela, Colombia, Ecuador, Peru, and Bolivia.

SUN BEAR

Smallest of all the bears, the sun bear averages 100 pounds and measures about four feet long. It keeps to the dense Southeast Asian forests of Sumatra, Borneo, the Malayan Peninsula, Myanmar, and Thailand.

GIANT PANDA

The giant panda makes its home in the high mountains of central China, where bamboo, its favorite food, is plentiful. The rare panda is confined to an area only 300 miles long and about 80 miles wide.

BIG BODIES

How would you describe a bear? Look carefully. Most bears have a large head with a long snout, small close-set eyes, and erect ears. Their heavily built body has short, thick limbs and a stumpy tail. And, yes, they are big and furry!

Talk about big! There once was a polar bear that weighed over 2,000 pounds and measured 11 feet long.

FANTASTIC FUR

Fairly uniform in color, bear fur can be either black, white, or many shades of brown. But several species have light-colored markings on their chest that accent their size when they rear up to fight or defend themselves.

▲ GRIN AND BEAR IT

Most bears have 42 teeth. Their sharp canines can tear flesh from a carcass, while their broad, flat molars allow them to grind down plants.

Unlike the claws of most cats, a bear's claws can't be pulled in when not in use.

KILLER CLAWS ▲

A bear's foot comes equipped with five long, curved claws. Bears use these sharp, all-purpose claws to mark or climb trees, dig for food, excavate their dens, rip apart prey, scratch, or defend themselves.

NEARSIGHTED ▶

Bears are built for seeing small things close at hand, such as berries and other food. In fact, they are fairly nearsighted and sometimes get so absorbed in eating that they don't see an approaching person. Hikers often whistle or wear bells to alert bears of their presence.

◀ BODY LANGUAGE

Bears not only use their body for movement, but also to communicate. A stare from a bear is a serious threat. But when a bear lowers its head, that means it wants peace. Bears also mark trees or other objects in their territory with their scent or claw marks.

NOSING AROUND

Smell is probably a bear's greatest sense. Like a bloodhound, it can accurately sniff out a trail where prey walked many hours before. It can also pick up a scent from the air and find the source miles and miles away.

FAST FEET

They may look slow and clumsy, but bears walk like people—on the soles of their feet, with heels touching the ground. Some are also fast runners. Brown bears can reach speeds of up to 40 miles per hour—faster than any Olympian sprinter and as fast as a greyhound!

STAYING COOL ▶

During the summer, bears have to stay cool, especially polar bears, which are built for very cold weather. They spread out and expose their massive body to the air or ice.

▶This sleepy polar bear cools itself off in some Arctic slush.

LEAVING THE DEN

When spring arrives, bears leave their den to search for food. During their first weeks outside, when the only available food may be grasses, herbs, and twigs, bears tend to lose weight. Adults also shed their thick coats so they'll be cooler in the summer months ahead.

In Alaska, ▶ this bear is enjoying a meal of blueberries.

HARVEST TIME

In the forest, as new foods ripen in late summer, the bear family gorges on berries, fruits, and nuts. They spend more and more time eating, storing up a thick layer of fat to provide energy and extra insulation during the long winter months.

The fruit of a rose, called ▶ a rose hip, is a tasty treat for a grizzly bear cub.

FINDING A MATE

For several months in the spring, bears leave their solitary habits behind to seek out a mate. Courtship may include vicious fights among competing males. Mating bears sometimes spend a few days together, but the males soon leave to seek out another female.

These two male grizzly bears are preparing to fight.

TO THE DEN

In the fall, bears begin their task of homemaking. Female polar bears dig their winter home in snowbanks. The Asiatic black bear makes a bed of fresh twigs on the forest floor. Grizzlies dig out homes underground, chewing off branches to build springy mattresses. Black bears find a denning space in a cave.

◀ A black bear mother and cub cuddle up in their den.

A black bear mother ▶ nursing her two little cubs.

WINTER BABIES

Cubs are born during the winter in the shelter of a den. Very tiny at birth, the cubs spend the first weeks of their lives nursing and sleeping.

Polar bear cubs snuggle ▶ into the warmth of their mother's fur.

READY FOR SLEEP

When a bear enters its winter den, it is fat, has a thick coat, and is ready for sleep. Body temperature lowers and heart rate decreases. Cubs that spend more than one season with their mother accompany her into the den, but otherwise a bear sleeps alone.

13

EATING EVERYTHING

Bears are omnivorous—they will gobble down just about anything in sight. And that may be the secret to their success—they are not fussy eaters and can find a tasty meal just about anywhere.

▼ Not great hunters, black bears eat mostly plant matter, including grass, berries, acorns, roots, and herbs.

A SEASONAL DIET

A bear's diet may change from season to season—the tender roots or shoots of spring plants, ripe summer berries and fruit, and acorns in the fall. In the spring, bears also eat trees, peeling away the bark to get at the inner layer, called *cambium*.

EATING MEAT

Bears are not the great killers many people think they are. They do catch and eat small animals, and some, like the polar bear, eat more meat than others. But when it comes to eating larger prey, bears mostly feed on animals that are already dead.

◀ On the coast of Alaska, this hungry grizzly attacks a razor clam.

14

FISHING
Alaskan brown bears are great at fishing. They grab fish in their mouth or pin them down with their front paws. They even leap from overhanging boulders and plunge into the water to nab a passing fish. Gathering at streams and rivers during the salmon run, brown bears may eat as much as 90 pounds of fish in one day!

▼ PATIENT HUNTER
The predatory polar bear has several hunting techniques. In one, called "still hunting," the bear sniffs out a seal's "breathing hole" and then may wait patiently for hours above it. When a seal surfaces for air, the bear instantly delivers a powerful blow, grabs with its sharp, pointed teeth, and hauls it out of the water.

▼ UNHAPPY CAMPERS
When a bear is around, nothing edible is safe. Campers come out of their tents in the morning to find packages of food ripped open, jars smashed, and coolers overturned. The best remedy is to buy "bear-proof" containers or hang the food out of reach.

IN THE DUMPS
Garbage dumps are an open invitation to hungry bears. As the bears lose their fear of people and become more dependent upon them for food, they may actually become more dangerous.

CUTE CUBS

A mother bear gives birth in her winter den to one or two babies that weigh only a few ounces. Covered with a thin, fuzzy layer of hair, they are blind and completely helpless. After surviving the winter on rich, fatty milk, bear cubs will leave the den in spring and go out into the world with their mother.

◀ Only 10 days old and weighing 30 ounces, these grizzly cubs will grow to about 150 pounds in their first year.

MOM KNOWS BEST ▶

When it comes to learning the secrets of bear life, a cub's only teacher is its mother. By following, watching closely, and imitating her actions, cubs learn everything they need to know—how to hunt, where to find berries or a fishing stream, how to dig for ants or get honey from a beehive.

KEEPING A DISTANCE ▲

A cub's worst enemy is another bear. If a cub comes too close to an adult male, it risks being attacked and killed. Mother bears have to be fiercely protective of their babies and do everything they can to keep them away from older males.

PLAYTIME ▶

Playing is an important part of a young bear's life. When playfighting, cubs will stand up and try to push one another off balance. But if play becomes too rough, a cub can stop every-thing by flattening its ears and giving out a low warning sound.

Although climbing is a fun kind of play, it's also a way to get at food and escape danger.

◀ LEAVING HOME

Some cubs remain with their mother for up to three years, denning with her in the winter. Others are on their own after a year. Once they leave, cubs may stay together for a few months or go their separate ways. They've learned the basics, and now it's time to live a bear's life.

FOUR LITTLE BEARS

Take a look at the spectacled, sun, sloth, and Asiatic bears. They're the smallest of all bears, and they are very unique.

◀ A mother sun bear and her cub.

SUN BEAR

The sun bear is the smallest of the bears— about 3 to 4 and a half feet long and 100 pounds. Some people try to make this little black bear a pet, only to discover later that it's uncontrollable. The sun bear is one of the most dangerous animals in its territory.

TROUBLEMAKER ▲

Of all the bears, the Asiatic black is most likely to make trouble with people living in its territory. It has been known to raid herds of cattle, sheep, and goats, and to destroy crops. It also has a reputation for being ill-tempered and has attacked people.

▼ A sun bear snoozing in a tree.

FRUIT LOVER ▶

If there's one thing the South American spectacled bear loves, it's fruit. After building a platform from branches high in a fruit-laden tree, it will settle in for days of feasting. When it has eaten all the fruit within reach, it picks up and moves to a new site.

▼ The spectacled bear.

LIVING VACUUM ▼

The sloth bear loves termites, its staple food. To get at them, it digs a hole in the nest, sticks its muzzle in, and blows violently to clean the surrounding area. Closing its nostrils, it then sucks in the insects. The sounds a sloth bear makes while vacuuming up its meal can be heard 200 yards away!

When playfighting, ▶ sloth bears can look pretty fierce. But unlike most bears, they actually like the company.

◀ TOP OF THE CLASS

Captive sun bears have proven their intelligence in amazing ways. One young bear figured out how to use its huge, curved claw as a key, unlocking a cupboard and taking out a sugarbowl. Another scattered rice from its dish to attract chickens, which it then killed and ate.

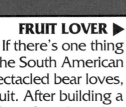

NORTHERN GIANTS

Amidst the ice floes of the Arctic Circle lives the polar bear—the king of the north. This bear reaches gigantic sizes, and does so by eating meat. A skilled hunter, the polar bear has been known to attack beluga whales, jumping on their back, then riding them under the sea.

MEAT EATERS

Polar bears live almost entirely on ringed seals. Other prey might include a walrus calf, a musk-ox, fish, or a whale. During the brief Arctic summer, they move onto land and eat whatever plants, small mammals, birds, and bird eggs they can find.

DOG-PADDLING

Almost invisible on the white ice, the polar bear can stalk a resting seal. Or, by using its webbed paws to "dog-paddle" towards its prey, it can dive underwater for as long as two minutes, then launch itself as far as eight feet into the air and land on the ice!

POLAR PALS

Instead of denning, male polar bears may stay active, hunting throughout the harsh winter. Sometimes they meet up with other polar bears and take time for a little fun. Playfighting is a way to develop their strength and hunting skills.

CURIOUS COAT

Perfectly insulated, the polar bear has a thick layer of fat under its skin and more fur than any other bear. Fur on the soles of its paws helps the bear grip ice. Surprisingly, polar bear fur is hollow. The hair collects light from the sun and channels the heat to the polar bear's black skin. Because the skin is black, it absorbs the heat.

A nap is a good way for polar bears to conserve energy in the cold Arctic.

SNOWY DENS

In the fall, females start digging their winter dens in the snowbanks. Warm air gets trapped inside, and drifting snow covers the opening. In late December or early January the female gives birth, usually to twins.

This polar bear cub stays warm inside its den.

MOM KNOWS BEST

When the polar bear family breaks out of the den in March or April, the cubs weigh about 22 pounds and have thick fur coats. For nearly two years they watch their mother closely, learning the hunting skills needed for survival.

ALL-AMERICAN

With its powerful body, the North American black bear can outrun a person, shinny up a tree with amazing speed, and easily break through dense underbrush in a forest. Although called a black bear, it comes in many colors, such as blue-black, brown, cinnamon, or even white.

▼ A cinnamon-colored black bear.

SIZING UP

An adult male black bear is about 4 to 6 feet long when fully grown and can weigh up to about 580 pounds. As with most bear species, males are considerably larger than females.

CURLING UP ▼

Black bears usually curl up for the winter in a cave. Some of them will dig a den under the roots of a large tree. If the trees have been logged out, they make beds on the ground amongst thick vegetation, raking up leaves and plants to lie on.

GHOST BEAR

Found only in a small area of British Columbia, Canada, the Kermode bear is the white version of a black bear. Also called "ghost bears," Kermode bears are so rare that few people have actually seen them.

◀ UP A TREE

When a black bear cub leaves the den, its claws are already well developed. The cub needs them, because every time the mother bear senses danger, she will chase her cubs into the nearest tree.

A black bear mother ▶
and her cub.

BARE SOLES

Bears that stay on the ground most of the time, like polar bears, have feet with hairy soles. But black bears, which spend much of their life in trees, have bare soles. Along with sharp, narrow, curved claws, bare soles make it easier for the black bear to climb.

MIXED MENU ▶

The black bear is a powerful swimmer and good fisher. On land, the bear flips over stones and decayed logs to find insects and grubs. It digs out burrows to reach small rodents. It also feeds on vegetation, such as berries, and loves honey.

A black bear taking a swim.

MIGHTY BEAR

Brown bears rank among polar bears as the largest of all bears. The heaviest yet recorded weighed more than 2,000 pounds. Perhaps the best-known brown bear is the mighty grizzly. "Grizzled" means partly gray, which perfectly describes the gray-tipped hairs of a grizzly's shaggy coat.

TOP BEAR ▲

Spectacular fights occur between big, male brown bears when they are courting and when they gather at rivers to fish for migrating salmon. If the challenged bear does not turn his head and back up, the two go at each other with vicious lunges, slapping and biting until one bear gives up.

THE BROWN FAMILY

One of the largest brown bears is the Kodiak, found only on Kodiak Island in southern Alaska. Other brown bears include the Siberian bear, the red bear of northern India and the Himalayas, the Manchurian bear, the horse bear of Tibet and western China, and the Hokkaido bear of Japan.

◄ HUMPBACK

Ranging in color from light cream to black, brown bears are sometimes confused with black bears. However, brown bears are larger, have round faces, and have a hump on their back. The hump is a mass of muscles that gives them added power for digging and fighting.

EVERY BITE

Grizzlies eat everything, including fungi, leaves, berries, roots, sprouting plants, insects, fish, and small mammals. When they find the carcasses of larger animals, like moose, elk, or livestock, they store the remains, returning again and again to the storage site until every last morsel is consumed.

AMAZING CLAWS

Grizzlies and other brown bears have enormous claws, which sometimes reach six inches in length. With these tools they do battle, dig, climb, handle food, and scratch. One very skilled grizzly was even seen handling a feather, turning it over and over in its paws.

▲ CUBSITTING

Grizzlies are not as solitary as was once thought. Female grizzlies will adopt motherless cubs and may even develop friendships. In the McNeil River area of Alaska, two females met one another almost every day and swapped cubs over an entire summer.

PANDA PALS

With its striking black-and-white image the giant panda cannot be mistaken for any other bear. This national treasure of China is one of the most popular animals visited at zoos.

BAMBOO, PLEASE ▼

A giant panda may spend much of its time sitting and tearing off the coarse leaves and stems of bamboo, its favorite food. It may also eat a little grass, some flowering plants, or raid a beehive for honey. A special "thumb" on its front paws helps the giant panda grasp bamboo stems. Unique among bears, this false thumb is made up of an elongated wrist bone.

SEVERE MEASURES

Because of hunting and loss of habitat, the giant panda is endangered. Symbol of the World Wildlife Fund, the giant panda has a population fewer than 1,000. It is in such danger of extinction, the Chinese government has decreed that anyone killing a giant panda may be sentenced to death.

The red ▶ panda

◀ BEAR OR RACCOON?

For many years scientists wondered if the giant panda is a bear or a relative of the raccoon. The giant panda has many similarities to the smaller red panda, which *is* a member of the raccoon family. However, today, scientists classify the giant panda as a bear.

26

LITTLE GIANT

Despite its name, the giant panda measures only 27 to 31 inches tall from the ground to its shoulders. It's about five to six feet from nose to rump. In most bear species, males are considerably larger than females, but all adult giant pandas are nearly the same size. It's almost impossible to tell them apart.

LOOKING FOR A MATE

During mating season, giant pandas find one another by scent and sound. To advertise their presence, they rub their scent glands against trees. The male vocalizes with an eerie call, and the female responds with a sheeplike bleat.

BLACK-AND-WHITE BABIES

At birth, giant panda cubs weigh a mere 3 to 5 ounces. Within weeks they have developed a light version of the striking black-and-white panda coat. In a year they are on their own, and their mother gives birth again.

27

BEARS AND PEOPLE

Bears are not so much *a* danger as they are *in* danger. In the early 1800s, one explorer traveling in Colorado saw over 200 grizzly bears in one day. Today, there are probably fewer than 70,000 grizzlies in all of North America. As people log wilderness areas and plant crops, bears lose habitat. Also, bears are still hunted.

STUDY BUDDY

Scientists study a bear's needs in order to help provide for its survival. However, studying bears in the wild is usually difficult because they are such shy animals, and scarce. Researchers sometimes tag bears with radio collars in order to keep track of their movements.

Visiting bear country in a bus is a good way to view wildlife while avoiding attacks.

▲ POLAR PROTECTION

Hunting polar bears for sport was once so popular that in 1965 people had to band together to help save this magnificent creature from extinction. Today, only native peoples in Greenland and Alaska may hunt polar bears for their own use.

DANCING BEAR

For centuries, people have used bears for entertainment. Bears have performed in circuses, street acts, the movies, and television. The ancient Romans used bears in their circuses, along with chariot races and warrior contests.

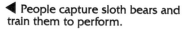

◀ People capture sloth bears and train them to perform.

SERIOUS ATTACK

Bear attacks on people are rare, but if people get too close, especially to a mother's cubs or to a bear's food, an attack is more likely. The bear will charge on all four legs, then strike with a bite or a claw.

Tours

A POPULAR IMAGE ▲

Cuddly bear characters are all around—in books, movies, and advertisements. One of the most popular images of all, Smokey the Bear, was created during World War II as an aid for fire prevention. Today, he is still at work reminding us with his slogan, "Remember, only you can prevent forest fires!"

THE TEDDY BEAR ▶

In 1902, President Teddy Roosevelt went hunting but had little success. So a captured black bear cub was brought out for him to shoot. The president refused, and the story touched the hearts of the people. Soon a small toy bear was created that became one of the most popular toys ever made—the "Teddy Bear."

▲ A black bear cub